Casa Italiana

Casa Italiana

Patrizia Catalano
Photographs by Henry Thoreau

RIZZOLI
NEW YORK

to Martina

Cover
Roberto Lucifero's House, Rome

Graphic design
Sottsass Associati: Mario Milizia and Chiara Fasoli

Layout
Antonietta Pietrobon

Editorial coordination
Caterina Giavotto

Editing
Roberta Garbarini

Translation
Angela Arnone

First published in the United States of America in 2002 by
Rizzoli International Publications, Inc.
300 Park Avenue South
New York, NY 10010

© 2002 by Rizzoli Libri Illustrati
Società Editoria Artistica SpA
Gruppo Skira
Photographs © 2002 Henry Thoreau

Library of Congress Control Number: 2002106885

ISBN: 0-8478-2481-0

Printed in Italy

Contents

Italian Interiors

Patrizia Catalano

Many images spring to mind when imagining a house in Italy. The Tuscan farmhouse on a Siena hilltop; the aristocrat's villa with its harmonious proportions, tiled roof, and classical gardens; the Mediterranean house, with whitewashed walls and scented jasmine on the terrace. A lovely Italy, enchanted, which now is to be found sadly more in our imagination than in everyday reality. Today it is more common to see prefabs created in the name of hygiene and efficiency. But standardization poses a problem: it is boring.

When I arrived at the Italian women's magazine *IO Donna* to edit the "Home" page, I wondered whether I should go for a varied and heterogeneous interpretation criterion. In particular, the objective I set myself was to seek out an original and contemporary Italian style and look for authentic houses, autographed by the personality of those who live there. I sought enthusiasts of the art of living, those intrigued by their surroundings, content to adhere to a personal and sometimes eccentric model. Perhaps this is the common thread that links the twenty-five stories gathered in this volume. Both famous and unheard of personalities, who used their own homes to affirm themselves, are featured. As I said, no style dominated. In fact, the goal was to find as much diversity as possible, from contemporary to classical, from eccentric to baroque.

The owners of these houses do share one thing: the need to leave one's mark on one's own nest. A number of affinities can be seen. For some, a house is a manifesto of their personal aesthetic. It may be an act of faith in modern and rationalist architecture, as in the case of the Roman architects Piero Sartogo and Nathalie Grenon, who are involved in twentieth-century culture and thus collect historic items, lamps, objects, textiles, and works of art, combining them with great harmony within the container they have designed.

Again in Rome, Roberto Lucifero does the same, declaring himself to be an artist and expert in ancient techniques. His house is a baroque theory, a sequence of wings and stage sets. Another recurrent theme is the house-museum. In Naples the designer Ernesto Esposito, who has collected contemporary art since he was a youth, asked the designer to provide him with a neutral container to house works of art that he changes continuously. Once again in Naples, the historian Vittorio Baratti creates a sequence of rooms with a layout quite similar to a nineteenth-century museum, where he houses seventeenth-century Neapolitan works of art and Capodimonte porcelain of the seventeenth and eighteenth centuries. Or maintain a house as if it were a work of art in itself, leaving intact the spirit of the era in which it was designed. This was the case with Villa Feltrinelli, which belonged to the historic Feltrinelli family: after twenty years of neglect it was restored to its ancient splendor thanks to the care and investment of its new owner.

A stone's throw from Cremona there is the atmosphere of the ancient Poor Claire convent, that has belonged to the same family for over a century, retaining its neoclassical charm thanks to the efforts made by the owners. On the other hand there are those who dabble in and interact with local culture to create a personal style. Fiora Gandolfi, in Venice, reinterprets the technique of Venetian stucco and decorates the house with the personal style of an artist. In Bari, in the Muratti quarter, the owners of an Umberto-period apartment use bold color choices and styles that reinforce the house's 1930s layout. An international style dominates in Milan, in the loft belonging to designer Rodolfo Dordoni and in the attic of Italo Araldi, a major figure in the city's fashion system. Last, but not least, the homes of artists: in Rome, the studio of Bruno Caruso, set up with the sophistication of a refined intellectual and, also in Rome, the house-theatre of Luciano Damiani, both furnished with set designer flair.

Our research began in Venice. This was not by chance. Venice is a city that has hosted and made famous two figures that are the models of the art of transforming their homes into paradigms of the art of living. They gave me a helping hand to search all of Italy and pursue a coherent theme. Mariano Fortuny was a master of style, born in Madrid and Venetian by adoption: he was the first of Italy's modern tourists. He lived in a seventeenth-century palazzo and instead of adapting to the taste that reigned in Venice at that time, he turned the rules on their head. He used the plan of the Venetian house and adapted it to the requirements of a painter, scenographer, textile designer, and photographer. Today we speak of Fortuny-style as if he had been an interior decorator. In truth Fortuny was a decorator only for his own personal pleasure and left the world an indelible legacy.

Another, more recent, example was Peggy Guggenheim. Her house in Dorsoduro (Palazzo Venier dei Leoni), was an example of contamination. The modern layout was desecration for a city like Venice, and throughout the 1950s and 1960s became the model for a glamorous and cosmopolitan lifestyle. The Guggenheim palazzo is a testament to her passions: a passion for modern art, for collecting, for parties and high society, for her dogs, and for her wardrobe. She created an eccentric place and that was the very reason for its charm: she created an environment that conformed to her own very personal requirements.

The book is organized in two sections. The first is a series of essays about houses where the sense of design is strong indeed, both in the case in which the owner is the direct artifice of the intervention, and also when an architect has been commissioned: either way, the concept of comfort is never betrayed in favor of aesthetic severity, but in fact supported by it.

The second section shows images that seek to fit together the puzzle of a strange landscape, that of a globalised vernacular, center of a memory of styles and eras that were subtracted from the necessity of a historic coherence, also thanks to a universe of technologies that render it perversely anachronistic. And their charm lies in this successful perversion, the sum of arcadia and media, seen as bizarre by the architect's eye and dear to that of the decorator, intellectual, and historian.

Houses in Focus

Henry Thoreau

The eye of the photographer is sensitive to space, swiftly perceives nuances, and sees combinations that escape the normal onlooker. And an image that depicts an interior is made up of space, which explains the relationship between objects, between light and objects, which is like incandescent liquid matter that like a tidal wave sweeps over walls, furniture, paintings, all those items that it swallows up and liquefies.

The photographer is a wizard. Once the houses have had their picture taken, they lose their identity, surprise their owners, like a portrait in which they do not recognize themselves. The camera is a magic box, and this is where the transformation—a miracle—occurs, which is repeated each time the alchemy of the image is perfect, like the blood liquefying in the hands of a priest.

And in the camera's little black box, which precedes the mirror, where the image filtered by the lens is projected, the infinite difference between what we imagine and what is really there can be perceived.

The space in houses, before a photographer's eye, multiplies like that of the enchanted castles of our childhood, rich in shadows and secret places, destined for fantastic encounters. Their true story no longer counts and each time the photographer falsifies the inexorable datum of truth. What counts is only the strange relationship that the objects have with the camera's black box, their way of posing for the camera, like narcissists at the mirror. The abyss, once again brought to life by the trickery of the image, thus unfolds before the eye of the camera, until its inevitable, final destiny, the magical "click" that forever fixes the form to the film, then reopens its gaze to other possible adventures.

And Italy does not lack adventures. Adventures of beauty and of emotions, which still catch us unawares, arrive from far away when the diaphragm of time opens, within houses and outside of them, too. So, back and forth, across the *bel paese* many things are discovered, but most of all happiness. I hope, and I wish, that some of this happiness will linger on the pages of this book, thanks to the love and intelligence of those who opened the doors of their homes and whom I thank for having understood and helped us in our project.

The Italian House: Comfort Meets Design

Shadow Play

A Retro House in Bari

The photo above shows the living area: a mirrored structure with console divides the sitting room from the dining area. Facing page: the bedroom. Old fabrics like the bedspread or modern like the curtains blend with the blue walls.

What can we say when we encounter a house that over time has safeguarded its identity? This is the case here in Bari, in the heart of the Muratti quarter. The apartment is on the top floor of an Umberto period house, enjoying a view of the port of Bari. At first sight this is not a building with a southern character. But that is a superficial impression. In reality it is very southern in its elegance, its measure, its charm. The striking element is the light: the contrast between the blinding luminosity of the exterior and the half-light of the interior is deliberate. The owner of the house is a partner in one of Bari's most important jewelry design galleries. She has opted for precise color choices with three sources of inspiration: the floor, in original turn-of-the-century marble-chip floor tiles, different in each room, with Art Deco–style geometrical motifs and in rather dark tones: gray, brown, black, sienna. The door and window frames are in late Art Nouveau style, with walnut structure. Lastly there is a high-vaulted ceiling, over seventeen feet, with handsome vaults for each room and plaster appliqués.

How is it possible to reconcile these three elements? If the tradition of Puglia were to be applied then, the instruction would be to whitewash everything. However, the owner of the house felt that by whitewashing she would have lost all these elements, so she followed the advice of a friend, who supervised the decoration and thought that some color was called for in order to create harmony. Hence the nougat-colored plastering of the entrance and hallway; the apricot color of the huge living room; the aubergine-colored Japanese straw in the small study; the oxblood tint in one of the children's rooms; burgundy in the study; and sea green in the master bedroom.

The combinations are perfect and the rooms have volume. In the furnishings there are many dark items, which give force and character to the house. In the drawing room there is a great panel that separates the dining area from the sitting area. One side of the panel is covered in mirrors and has an incorporated black wooden cocktail cabinet. An ancient Japanese rice paper painting covers the other side. The living area is filled with sofas, armchairs, and a dormeuse, all upholstered in important fabrics, predominantly black and sage green velvet. The bedrooms and study have excellent quality built-in shelves. They are fitted into the niches and finished with wood frames and curtained glass doors, recovering the house's historic spirit. The only element that breaks away is the bathroom, which has been totally rebuilt and has 1930s inspiration boiserie in variegated marble and a handsome play of arches.

Top: the corridor. Bottom: the entrance, with an art deco table, 1930s Seguso glassworks Venetian vase, and cement mosaic tile floors. Facing page: detail of the living area, a mirrored room divider with incorporated cocktail cabinet, by the architect Antonio Nobile.

*The house is a sonata of dark tones. The gray wallpaper in
the library harmonizes with the burgundy corduroy upholstered
settee and the 1920s wood and black velvet easy chairs.
Facing page: the library again, with a glass and wood bookcase.
The doors are lined with antique cotton curtains to protect the books.*

The master bathroom, with green and black variegated marble paneling. The bathtub is set in an arched niche, shielded by a tinted glass partition. Facing page: the bedroom. The house is characterized by original plaster applications, Japanese straw wallpaper in dark tones, and marble-chip floor tiles with geometric designs.

A Whiter Shade of Contemporary

An Attic in Milan

Italo Araldi, one of the leading figures in the Milanese fashion business, owns a top floor apartment in Milan in a modern building from the 1960s. When he commissioned the house from the firm of architects Caruzzo Rancati Associati, he asked them to capture as much light as possible, to create unusual spaces that were open but laid out in areas with different functions. From the entrance it is obvious that the architects were listening to the client: a galaxy of white light welcomes the visitor. The house is an elongated space, divided into several zones: the living area, with a veranda that looks out onto terraces turned into a hanging garden; the dining area, that accesses a kitchen and bathroom; the sleeping area, split, in turn, into a studio; a bedroom; and a bathroom. Mirrored exactly by the latter area there is a door that leads into a second apartment—also restructured by Caruzzo Rancati—which is the home of a close friend of the owner.

These are two independent apartments, but with spaces that may be shared. "A sort of extended and very relaxed family," comments Araldi. If the distribution of space hinges on harmony to create continuity between one area and another, the same can be said of the choice of materials. The walls and built-in cupboards are cream, finished in Mantua stucco, with a pleasing satin effect. The floor, in squares of ivory-colored stone, is very opaque. "I find that an opaque effect creates a softer and more homogenous atmosphere: I was looking for a great white container with an all-embracing effect."

There is little furniture, but it is carefully selected. The architects designed much of it. The wall cupboards that conceal every possible thing have two-foot square doors. The kitchen fittings are in steel, the professional type. The living room furniture is in milk-white corian, housing a sophisticated hi-fi system. Finally, the bathroom is finished in variegated marble, including the fittings. The limited items of furnishing are carefully chosen and they are mainly pieces designed by masters of design such as Charles Eames, Arne Jacobsen, and Marcel Breuer. There are no pictures on the walls, no books on show, and very few ornaments. The walls are interrupted by one or two elements: a ceramic art nouveau fireplace bought in Paris and surmounted by a "hi-tech" painting, a plasma TV set. Even the accessories are cut right to the bone. Araldi brought with him from a previous home an early-twentieth-century Italian-design brass table lamp with six arms of the 1940s. The collection of interesting artifacts includes early-twentieth-century Venetian vases, eighteenth-century Burmese heads, and a twelfth-century wooden votive statue, also from Burma. The space closes around the hanging garden, with a carefully tended lawn, and almond and olive trees.

A completely restructured house with a large veranda living room, divided into various zones. Facing page: a detail of the living area. Mantua stucco walls, light stone floors and Nordic style armchairs designed by Arne Jacobsen in 1958, upholstered in lilac fabric.

The house has three terraces with fruit trees and a lawn. Facing page: a studio characterized by a ribbon window and a collection of vases from the 1920s and 1930s.

In this image the "lounge chair" designed by Charles Eames in 1957, a corian table and container by the architects Caruzzo Rancati, a nineteenth-century Burmese statue, and early-twentieth-century Venetian glass items. Facing page: the dining area is furnished with a white lacquered modular cabinet and an industrial kitchen. On the first floor there are more items of historic design: a table by Eero Saarinen and chairs by Marcel Breuer.

Top: one of the house's two bedrooms whose slightly curved walls conceal a wardrobe area. Bottom, and facing page: the master bathroom, with its art deco mirror and shower area with gold and brown tiles, and basin cabinet in speckled marble.

The Warrior's Repose

A House, a Testament: Casa Carlo Mollino, Turin

This house is certainly the most unusual of those that Carlo Mollino has made his home in Turin. Unlike most of his architecture, here the architect has attempted to combine classicism with contemporary. The result is a testament-house where each object, even the most seemingly futile, acquires a sense of aesthetics and design. The apartment is on the first floor of a building dated 1888. It was the home of Gigi Chessa and then of Francesco Menzio, both painters of "The Turin Six" group, before passing to Carlo Mollino in 1960. From 1960 to 1965 Mollino renovated the apartment, gutting it completely and rebuilding it from scratch.

Even before getting past the threshold, the front door is striking, as an oval mirror reflects whoever is about to go in. One is shocked to be met by one's own portrait, signed by Mollino, but this is only the first of many illusionist tricks in store. Closing the door behind us we realize that the trick is repeated on the back of the door. The apartment has a corridor along its entire length and on the right—which looks out over the river—are the great living room and Mollino's bedroom, and on the other side the kitchen and bathroom. At the back, there is another bedroom. The entrance is separated from the living room by Japanese-style wings. The floor contrasts with this Japanese atmosphere as it is tiled in Vietri majolica. Opposite the Japanese door we see, the first

of the house's four great pier-glasses. The mirror is one of the materials that the architect uses frequently; with antiqued effect it serves to dilate space and acts as a scenographic element.

In the living room a contrasting effect has been created between classic and modern, between elements of industrial production and others that are handmade. The interior falls into three sections: the area around the french window that opens out onto the terrace, the sitting room, and the dining area. The most interesting is the zone that leads out onto the terrace. A play of doubles that emphasizes the access to the exterior: two mirror elements frame the french window; above there is a bronze appliqué, beneath it a pair of shells set on two benches, in turn preceded by two Indian braziers in the shape of a mythological lion. The composition concludes with a zebra skin and a Venini crystal chandelier.

The sitting room, in black leather, has a fireplace on the far wall, also covered in mirrors, designed by Mollino. The wall is decorated with tree-patterned photographic paper used as wallpaper. On the ceiling is a gigantic faux Japanese rice-paper lantern; its twin hangs in the dining area. Along the corridor with its fitted wardrobes, one reaches the bedroom. The tiny room hinges on the contrast between eroticism and romanticism: the sensuality of a leopard stripe wallpaper, velvet draperies, slightly faded but originally antique pink; the carpet blending with the framed butterfly collection; and the severe single bed, and the lace dresses that the architect used to buy personally at Sangallo in Switzerland, for his models. But these girls never entered this room: they stayed in the room next door where the gentleman architect immortalized them with his mythical Polaroid.

The sitting room furniture of the Casa Mollino living area. The wall is decorated with tree-patterned photographic paper used as wallpaper, a large pier-glass with antique glass, and an embedded and oversized marble fireplace made to one of Mollino's own designs. A small clay statue accentuates the size of the fireplace. Facing page: a detail of the living room console.

In the corridor, the floor is made of Vietri majolica. The front door has a double oval mirror and was redesigned by Mollino. On the left, one of the house's four great pier-glasses, with console.

A Japanese-style wing, created by the architects
Campo and Graffi, divides the large living area from
the entrance. In the background the sitting room in
the living area, with a capitonné sofa by the architect
Osvaldo Borsani.

Top: the central living area. The french window that leads
to the terrace overlooking the river is characterized by a series
of symmetrical elements: two pier-glasses with bronze
applications, below, a pair of shells set on two benches which,
in turn, are preceded by two Indian braziers, modeled as two
mythological lions. The composition closes with a zebra skin.
Below: a detail against the Japanese panel. Facing page: another
view of the living area.

A 1970s Fornasetti screen in the bedroom. Facing page: the dining room. In the background, the pier-glass with console and the tree-patterned photographic paper. In the foreground a Mollino oval table and armchairs by Eero Saarinen.

In the bedroom, a mounted butterfly collection creates a contrast with the speckled wallpaper.
Facing page: the light-colored wood bed is protected by white and faded pink draperies. In the photos are several items of ladies' clothing that Mollino bought for his models.

Mollino has had an oval mirrored door fitted between the bathroom and the guest bedroom. Facing page: the bathroom tiled with Vietri majolica.

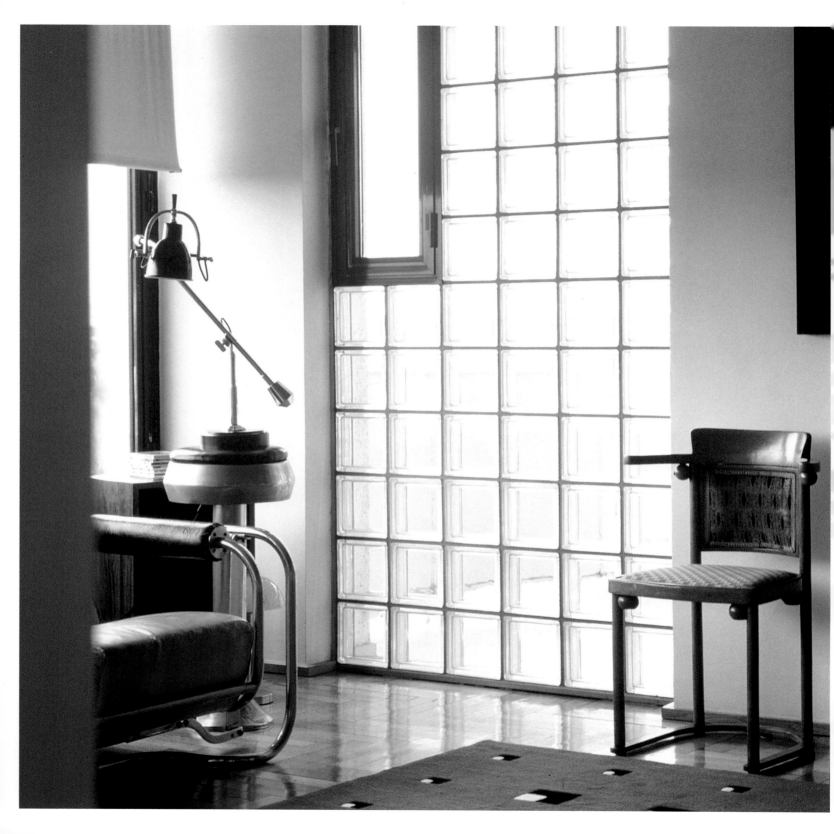

A Modern Effect

The Home of Piero Sartogo and Nathalie Grenon in Rome

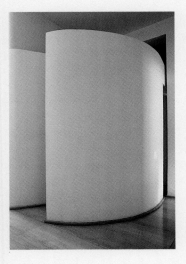 

A house may have many incarnations. This one is just such a case: it was first an apartment lived in by a father who was a lawyer and then a son who is an architect, with his family.

The son in question is Piero Sartogo, who runs one of Rome's busiest and most prestigious architecture firms with his wife, Nathalie Grenon. After many years spent in a Roman apartment in the historic center, on the top floor of a baroque building with a lovely terrace—ideal for hosting dinners—Piero Sartogo decided to return to the house of his youth. Paradoxically this was a return to modernity, a house that was actually designed in the 1930s by Cesare Pascoletti, an architect in vogue at that time, who gave the building a decidedly rationalist style. The interior, however, mimicked the traditional typology of a middle-class apartment, with rooms leading one into the other.

The couple decided to turn the previous layout on its head, ordering a massive renovation that included the structural elements, thus creating

a very functional apartment that could provide for the necessities of a large family with children.

The house covers about 1,150 square feet and is divided into a vast living area, a sleeping area, and a zone for facilities. The living area has a sitting room where all possible walls were demolished and is organized as an open space, like that of a traditional house. It is a similar concept to that of a loft with an open, fluid plan that looks out onto the city through huge windows and semi-transparent glass blocks framed in concrete.

Traces of the past have not been wiped out. Quite the opposite, in fact. The outlines of the old walls can be seen on the flooring, highlighting the structure of columns and square beams that cut across the space.

The meticulous renovation project, which covered even the tiniest details, is enhanced by an equally refined choice of furniture. Apart from a series of items designed by Nathalie Grenon, there is also a collection of modern pieces. From original 1930s Viennese chairs by Josef Hoffman to the bookcases designed for Le Corbusier's Maison du Brésil, at Paris University in the 1950s by Charlotte Perriand, to a black iron-and-wood table by Jean Prouvé. Distributed throughout the house there is an extremely sophisticated collection of lamps, mainly by early-twentieth-century American designers. The same quest for items of furniture can be seen reflected in the works of art. In the house we find works by John Bal, Giulio Paolini, Urs Lüthi, Lucio Fontana, Tano Festa, and many others. The bedrooms are spacious and informal. In particular, in one of the two children's rooms there is a table designed for children by Grenon: the table changes height as the child grows.

Above, two details in the access area, created by the architects Piero Sartogo and Nathalie Grenon in the family home. Facing page: a detail of the living room. The windows have been modified with one section in glass blocks and metal frames, and transparent glass. In the foreground a small Beidermeyer chair. Following page: an overall view of the living area. The walls have been removed to create an open plan.

When they knocked out the walls, the architect couple left traces of the past structure: outlines of the old walls can still be seen on the flooring. Facing page: modern items of furniture and pieces designed by Nathalie Grenon and Piero Sartogo. In the foreground the bookcase designed by Charlotte Perriand in the 1950s for Le Corbusier's Maison du Brésil in Paris.

A work by Giulio Paolini, comprising two plaster busts.
Facing page: an original Jean Prouvé writing desk in iron
and wood, and a Walter Gropius leather armchair.

Chic References

A Villa in Posillipo

The house enjoys a view across the seas of Posillipo. In this image we see a house with a pagoda tower, a typical example of the eclectic architecture in vogue at the turn of the twentieth century. Facing page: a detail of the entrance to Casa Baratti. A nineteenth-century Neapolitan table holds a collection of seventeenth- and eighteenth-century Capodimonte heads and statuettes.

Posillipo is the gentle, poetic soul of Naples, an out-of-town territory in a chaotic, tumultuous metropolis. The quarter has a permanent holiday feel, the houses along the tortuous coast road mould themselves to the outline of the coastline. The curious and eccentric figures who live here have made their houses the epitome of "Neapolitanness." One such figure is the art collector and scholar Vittorio Baratti, a refined gentleman of advanced years who lives in an eighteenth-century villa on a cliff top overlooking the sea. Baratti's apartment occupies the entire main floor of the house and includes a magnificent terraced garden that offers a panorama of the enchanting Gulf of Naples. But if the garden embraces all the sunny, joyous elements of the Parthenopean city, with its rare succulent plants, lemon trees, jasmine, bougainvillea, and sculptures set into the walls, the interior of the apartment has an obscure charm. Protected by shutters that filter the light and cast extraordinary beams of radiance, the house is more reminiscent of an old museum where the objects

have not yet found a precise location than of a home in the traditional sense.

The entrance is through a room that is always in half-light and two large ebony tables display a rare collection of Capodimonte items that date from the sixteenth to the twentieth century, accompanied by archaeological finds and vintage photographs. Continuing into the living area one gets a sense of the Neapolitan version of comfort that is unique. The sofas are rigid and severe, just as they should be in a museum-house, set against the walls and surmounted by works in the local baroque style. The structure is in wood, with armrests carved into dragon heads; the upholstery is in faded cardinal red velvet that blends wonderfully with the arabesque motif on the majolica that is used for flooring throughout the house, all produced by the famous Giustiniani kiln.

The rooms that face out onto the garden are large and luminous, furnished with antique furniture including a handsome bed in Neapolitan wrought iron of the 1800s and some contemporary items. This more private zone also contains expert collector's items such as a work depicting Raimondo di Sangro, prince of San Severo, and an intriguing collection of skulls. The son's room is definitely less formal. The eighteenth-century atmosphere is played down by a series of graphics and illustrations on the walls.

The bathroom and kitchen are unusual. The kitchen is in the oldest part of the house, located in the highest section of an ancient cistern, and has a severe feel to it. It is snobbishly furnished in shabby items that include an enameled four-ring gas cooker and a dish rack that displays a series of early-twentieth-century aluminum saucepans and lids that are still in use. The bathroom, on the other hand, resembles a grotto and the barrel-vaulted ceiling emphasizes an archaic and mysterious air.

The house includes historic pieces grouped together
in a deliberately casual way: from the nineteenth-century
wardrobe with mirror doors to the eighteenth-century writing
desk, and the nineteenth-century Neapolitan iron bed frame.

A dark wood sofa with armrests carved with dragon heads and upholstered in cardinal red velvet. Above, a seventeenth-century Neapolitan painting.

*Slivers of light filter through the shutters and project
across the walls of the house. The flooring and the fixtures
are in original eighteenth-century* boiserie. *The majolica
is from the Giustiniani workshop, at one time the most
famous in this region.*

The house is not laid out in a traditional way. Each room is a small museum, with study tables, works and archaeological items scattered almost everywhere. In this image, a detail of two gesso pieces and an iron sculpture of a serpent.

The kitchen is deliberately spare. White, luminous, and lacking decorative elements, it contrasts with the style of the rest of the house. Like many of the other rooms, it looks out onto the garden.

A guest room with nineteenth-century furniture
and an iron headboard with stylized serpent motif.
The serpent and the skull are two themes dear
to Vittorio Baratti.

The bathroom is the oddest room in the house. Totally windowless, it was created in the same yellow tufa that was used to construct the rest of the building. The barrel-vaulted ceiling emphasizes the archaic, mysterious atmosphere.

1970s Restyling
A Glass and Cement Home on the Torinese Hillside

Carlo Ferrari, a well-known restauranteur, says that living is an art and he has restructured a villa on the Torinese hillside that practices what he preaches: no-hassle living, the best he can afford. Ferrari's dream was to create a place where he could wind down after a hard day of work. For this project he chose an unusual house: "Turin is full of period villas. But it is rare to find an example of modern architecture."

This house dates back to the 1970s and was designed by Carlo Graffi, a renowned architect who worked for years with Carlo Mollino. The brutalist style that hallmarks the villa is typical of that time: exposed concrete, daring lines, severe angles, and ribbon windows set into the long sides of the house.

Over the years the villa has been revamped many times and Ferrari asked the architect Roberto Tornetta to retrieve its lost *esprit*. Tornetta lived and worked for many years in Miami, as did the owner of this villa, and he sought to safeguard the house's authenticity. He simply restored it by eliminating all interior walls and exposing the structure. Then he brought to light details that had been concealed, such as the great portholes that illuminate the basement, typical of that period, and maintained as much as was possible the materials of the time, like the texturized ceramic tiles and the red brick, used on the exterior.

The house has a main floor, which is a split-level open space, with a sitting room, studio, cinema zone, and an open kitchen, plus a room for guests and services. The upstairs is dedicated to the sleeping area. No doors here either: one passes from the bedroom to the bathroom and the dressing room. On the top floor there is a terrace that offers a panorama view of Turin.

Although the exterior has retained its original bunker aspect, the interior is the unchallenged reign of eclecticism. The walls alternate from pistachio green to canary yellow and vermilion, and the floor is made of bamboo. For the bathrooms a cobbled *boiserie* contrasts with an acid-yellow shower wall. The furnishings, too, are extremely liberal, with a prevalence of Italian and American art deco pieces. Leopard stripes are a feature of the house, used in both the owner's headboard upholstery and in the two extra large carpets used in the dining and sitting areas.

There is also a life-size image of the pop star Madonna, inside the carmine red laminated elevator, and the portrait of a pasha in a prominent position in the high-tech kitchen designed by the architect. The kitchen features a statement on the wall: *I want no trouble.*

The architect Roberto Tornetta undertook the restyling and for the ground floor opted for pressed bamboo flooring. The walls are predominantly ecru, except for those where a green and acid yellow checkerboard effect has been applied.

*The kitchen is a large space cadenced by ribbon
windows that look out onto the garden and courtyard.
The hi-tech kitchen is by Roberto Tornetta.*

*Two Charles Eames lounge chairs with teak frames flank
the fireplace to create a symmetrical effect. In the center
a leopard skin rug and a 1940s American alarm clock.*

Upstairs the owner of the house has his bedroom, wardrobe,
and bathroom, which is en suite *from the bedroom.*
The dappling motif on the rugs is repeated on the headboard.

Exotic Byzantine

Eccentricity in a Venetian House

Houses, we know, are the mirror of those who live in them. However, it is very difficult to describe the personality of Fiora Gandolfi. Journalist, writer, artist and stylist of refined fashion collections, Fiora is also known for her eclectic style and for her extremely personal reinterpretation of Venetian style. The building dates back to the 1400s and has a Gothic plan. Although it does not look out onto the Grand Canal, it did belong to illustrious Venetian families: Cavazza, Foscari, Mocenigo. Like many of the other mansions in Venice, the house had its name: Casa Mocenigo delle Zogge. "Zogge" in Venetian means jewels or precious stones, and in fact, the house was the home of branches of the Mocenigo family who traded in gems arriving from the Orient.

Apart from its ancient origins the house is striking for its position: it is anchored like a wherry amidst the three canals, which is unusual for Venice. The apartment is on the second floor of the house.

The photo shows a detail of the portego with sketches, lithographs and oils on the walls, and period furniture decorated by Fiora Gandolfi. Facing page: the kitchen with exposed brickwork, a collection of North African amphorae, Bassano ceramics and an eccentric lamp created with drawings and messages from friends.

The previous tenant was a pharmacist who had opted for a typical Venetian style of stuccoes, gilt, and Venetian plaster. The new owner reinterpreted the essence of Venice with more modern criteria. The entrance is a loggia with stone parapet and Gothic windows, laid out as a veranda; the light that filters from the colored glass creates a pleasing kaleidoscopic effect. Next one finds the *portego*, the true fulcrum of patrician homes in Venice, once the great corridor leading off to the various rooms (inhabited by different families) and used as a ballroom. Now it is used as a living area, with dining and work tables, a library, and lounge. The furniture here is chiefly salvaged and repainted by the lady of the house with decorations that mimic the Venetian plaster concept.

The house has two sitting rooms: one is more aristocratic, with stuccoes, mirrors, and frescoes, furnished in shades of cream and beige, with carpet covering the floor of the entire room designed by the artist herself; the other is rather more informal, in tones of green and orange, furnished with a dresser that houses exquisite Bassano pottery. The kitchen, formerly a barrel vaulted chapel, is the only room in the house with exposed brickwork. The bedroom, full of textiles and carpets bought during numerous trips to the Far East, is worthy of Scheherazade: damask cushions, generous curtains on the windows, carpets made by North African nomads laid one over the other, and a canopy finished with tapestries. The bathrooms are charming boudoirs with Venetian glass that match the rosy shades of the walls and mirrors. Finally, the artist's studio, which comprises two rooms, one opposite the other: in one room Fiora concentrates on the cerebral part of her work, writing, and developing; in the other, the artist expresses her creative spirit freely through cloth, ribbon, textiles, and items of clothing scattered as in a fairy tale.

The portego *houses the dining area, the lounge, and the library. In this image, the dining area with a Frattino style fabric covered table and period chairs. In the foreground, above, the Moroccan brass lantern chandelier.*

The rooms are set around the portego.
*In this image the TV rooms. The ceiling
and the wallpaper were decorated
by Fiora Gandolfi. The Venetian
handcrafted dressers of the late 1800s
use colored fabric weave.*

*The stucco room has original eighteenth-century decorations,
mirrors, and frescoes. On the floor a large rug decorated by
Fiora Gandolfi with the initials of her husband, Helenio Herrera,
a famous soccer coach who died several years ago.*

For the bedroom the owner of the house was inspired by Scheherazade. A four-poster bed with an organza canopy is at the center of a room overflowing with textiles: from the brocade on the studio couch to the Moroccan fleece blankets and kilim rugs. Facing page: a corner of a terrace that overlooks the canal.

The Art Gallery
The House-Gallery of a Neapolitan Stylist

Ernesto Esposito's house in Naples is in the center
f the city. It is an apartment located in an eighteenth-
century building. The house was renovated by
the architects Ennio Radogna and Paolo Colantuoni,
who erased every trace of the original style with
interventions of undoubtedly contemporary style.
There was a definite reason for this: Esposito, an
internationally famous designer known for his shoe
collections, wanted to give space to his prestigious
collection of contemporary art, which he began
to put together at an early age when he frequented
the Amelio Gallery. The apartment has a square
plan and so avoids the traditional structure of many
small rooms to adopt an airy solution quite similar
to an open space. Doors are done away with,
except for bathrooms, as the architects preferred
a fluid plan, with no actual barriers, but rather
movable partitions. To emphasize this feature
of the house as an art gallery, a light wooden floor
was chosen, with totally white walls and a slightly
lowered ceiling.

The living area, split down the middle by
a partition wall, includes a sitting room with a white
leather sofa that does not interfere with the many
works of art on the walls, while the tables are
historic pieces from Memphis. The study-library,
which separates the living area for the sleeping area,
is a system of wall shelving in satin-finished steel,
while the bedroom has built-in wardrobes and
an upholstered bed as its basic furnishings. The
kitchen and bathrooms also bear the designer stamp.
The kitchen is dominated by an industrial-type
satin-finished steel system, with a bar-style table
and chairs in curved beech. Vitrified tessellas
of a multicolored mosaic contrast with the
white design porcelain fittings in the bathrooms.

But the house would be just about characterless
without its works of art scattered everywhere,
bathrooms and kitchen included: in the sitting
room the most prestigious, including *I Cerchi* by
Ugo Rondinone, a gigantic *Stalactite* by Sol Lewitt,
a huge photograph by Clegg & Guttman that shows
the owner of the house against a fake Santa Chiara
chapel; also in the living area, a Donald Baechler
portrait and a sculpture by Haim Steinbach
with shoes designed by Esposito himself and
Capodimonte plates; in the kitchen, *Miss American
Legion* by the pop artist Mel Ramos, dated 1965;
in the bedroom, a color photo by the American
Jack Pierson; in the study-library, works by
Cindy Sherman, Peter Halley, and Michelangelo
Pistoletto; in the corridor work by Dan Flavin;
and an impressive CD collection, as the host,
a typical Neapolitan, comments "you can't live
without music."

*Ernesto Esposito's house was designed
to host his prestigious collection
of contemporary art. Facing page: the
living room. The sitting room furniture
in the center of the room is in leather,
wicker, and steel, an homage to
rationalism. Wall decorations include a
huge photograph by Clegg & Guttman,
showing the owner of the house against
a fake Santa Chiara chapel. In the
foreground, a work by Sol Lewitt.*

In the living area a work by Ugo Rondinone and one of Ettore Sottsass' Memphis tables. Facing page: the hi-tech kitchen, in steel, and, on the wall: Miss American Legion *by Mel Ramos.*

The living room is a neutral container, with white walls and light wood flooring. A brick wall is used as a wing to divide the lounge from the living area.

*Next to the guest bathroom,
finished with vitrified mosaic tiles,
a work by Cindy Sherman.
Facing page: a masculine bedroom.
Above the bed, with its Scottish
bedspread, a work by Peter Schoef.*

Roman Grandeur
Architecture and White Telephones in the Capital

The Serena family settled in the Parioli quarter of Rome in 1937. Their modern-style house was still surrounded by sheep tracks with dry stone walls and it was quite common to see the flocks strolling past. Today this has changed: the piazza where the building is located boasts rationalist and modern buildings, and is a point of reference for the refined Roman middle class.

Let us begin in the living room. The corridor looks out onto the hall of the house, which is an ample, windowless anteroom that outlines the architectural philosophy of the Busiri-Vici family who designed the house. Niches, wooden paneling, sliding doors, are several of the recurring features, combined with the taste for symmetry and a quest for precious materials. The floor is covered in light-colored marble, repeated in the niches that house works of art. In the hall a marble and brass fireplace faces an oil painting by Ippolito Caffi, dated 1853. The reception room is cadenced by windows and two sliding doors that lead into a small drawing room, library and study, and to the dining room. The reception room has not been modified in any way. The niches with glass and brass doors house Capodimonte items, the three grisailles depict Love and Psyche, the sofas are in antique pink and sage green. One of the most prominent antique items is an eighteenth-century Neapolitan console.

The drawing room that precedes the library repeats the decorative elements of the reception room, while the study is completely different. An elegant oak *boiserie* houses the bookcases that contain a collection of antique volumes. In the center, symmetrical to the writing desk, also in oak, there is a map of Roman europe in polychrome marble, illustrating the empire at the time of Trajan. Crossing back over the reception room one reaches the dining room.

On either side of the door there are two niches containing eighteenth-century Neapolitan porcelain and, farther down, two radiator shields in the form of a female silhouette, a decorative work signed by Assia, the Russian wife of Andrea Busiri-Vici, who decorated many Roman houses at the time. Two brass consoles cadence the room's symmetry, while the center is dominated by the star of the show, a marble-topped table with a brass structure. The bedrooms retain a glamorous flair, with pear wood and parchment furniture. The kitchen and bathrooms have an early rationalist touch, however. The former has crimson lacquered wood fittings and the latter are in black-and-white marble, with gray mosaic inserts and several details such as the radiator in chrome and the shower with a huge showerhead that is now back in fashion.

Above right, an eighteenth-century Neapolitan console with a pier-glass of the same period, holding 1920s cups and candelabras. Facing page: the drawing room has several sitting areas in pastel tones and flowered patterns. In the background, one of the three grisailles on the theme of Love and Psyche.

The dining room dominated by cream tones for the walls and carpeting, boasts
a brass and marble table in the center of the room, designed by the architects
Busiri-Vici. The sliding door closes it off from the drawing room. One can also see the
two niches with radiator covers designed by Assia Busiri-Vici. On the facing page,
one of the two consoles in the dining room and in the niche, an ancient Chinese vase.

The hall features a fireplace in marble and brass; the same type of marble has been used for skirting and door frames. Two 1930s armchairs flank the fireplace. Facing page: another view of the hall.

The kitchen, in white lacquered wood, is a rare example of early rationalist design, once again by the Busiri-Vici couple. Facing page: a folding door divides the lounge from what was Adelchi Serena's studio, finished in oak. In the background, the boiserie with its polychromatic marble map of the Roman empire at the time of Trajan.

Southern Charm

A Historic Farmhouse, Puglia

In the photo above, a detail of the lounge: an old 1920s sofa, upholstered in a striped fabric, and a classic English easy chair. Facing page: the retro style dining room with Italian nineteenth-century dresser and table, Thonet chairs, and 1930s chandelier.

Puglia is scattered with farmhouses. The one featured here is occupied by a young Pugliese couple who are in love with their homeland and, when they were newlyweds, decided to restore this farmhouse that had belonged to their ancestors. They were determined to turn it into a working farm. The structure is very beautiful, simple, archaic, and, in some ways, is reminiscent of Mexican constructions, with a few baroque details such as the small chapel front, the well, and the balconies of the main house. The apartment is a homage to the bygone nineteenth century, to the tradition, altogether southern, of patrician houses whose virtue lay in simple furnishings and a wealth that was never too obvious.

The house was restored rather than restructured. It belonged to paternal grandparents and the young owners thought it was beautiful just the way it was. Even unavoidable alterations, such as central heating or the renovation of bathrooms and plumbing, were all carried out in a manner that would not alter the magic of the place. The old oak doors and ceramic doorknobs were recovered, then painted in opaque white, and the same was done to the window frames. None of the shutters has been changed: a local carpenter searched for identical shutters and integrated those into the house.

The spirit of Puglia is white. The strong, external light is filtered by the shutters, but the walls must be white. By contrast, the floor is in turn-of-the-century marble-chip tiles that create a natural carpet of geometrical and floral motifs throughout the house. The items of furniture are few and carefully selected. In the hall, two turn-of-the-century walnut chairs and a console in the center of the room are the only pieces present here. In the living room one finds several small armchairs and a nineteenth-century sofa with walnut root structure, interspersed with benches and bentwood café seats. The dining room is characterized by a handsome walnut table and dressers of the same period that contain a collection of Grottaglie pottery with late-nineteenth-century decorations. On the mantelpiece there is a collection of vases from Empoli in blue crystal and hung in the center of the room, an original 1930s lamp made in Tuscan kilns.

The bedrooms have an old-fashioned look. There are handmade brass and wrought iron beds, 1920s walnut and walnut root bedside cabinets and commodes, and lace bedspreads and curtains handed down through generations of the family. The only deviation from the decor is in little Betta's room, with dolls and toys everywhere. There is no garden. Or rather not in the official sense of the word. There is a closed kitchen garden, with dry stone walls and citrus trees, medlars, and almonds. Nearby there is the olive garden with an old olive tree that has an incredibly wide and contorted trunk, named the "Baron" and said to be one of the oldest trees in Puglia.

The farmhouse is characterized
by early-twentieth-century
decorated marble-chip floor tiles
and the star-vaulted ceilings.
Bottom: another
view of the dining room.
Facing page: one of the
bedrooms with a traditional
late-nineteenth-century
lacquered iron bedframe.

The farmhouse is fully operational.
Top: above the massive structure
of the oil mill. Bottom: a wing that houses
all the agricultural equipment. Facing page:
the well, and in the background, the dry stone
wall that protects the citrus grove.

Joyous Informality

Marchioness Carignani's Home, Trieste

Casa Carignani is a 1920s villa in Trieste. The house, a stone's throw from the port area, does not look out directly onto the street as it is protected by a solid stone wall tinted in mustard yellow that is reminiscent of some early-twentieth-century Viennese vases. The layout is that of a classic Italian villa on two floors, with a great marble staircase that leads upstairs and a handsome Italian garden at the back of the house, looking out to sea.

The house is interesting and essentially reflects the owner's style, which is refined and informal, tending to an accumulation of objects so that each room has at least one collection that sets it apart. The living room is large and very luminous, with walls covered in golden yellow fabric and the floor in bottle green carpeting completely covered in oriental rugs of all sorts and sizes. The living area is split into three zones: in the center there is a sitting room, with a series of damask velvet sofas facing out onto the terrace and the garden beyond. Facing the entrance, on the right, there are sofas and armchairs scattered around a neoclassical marble fireplace, and opposite we see the dining area, with an illusion of space created by a wall covered in eighteenth-century mirror tiles. The furniture is not of any particular style and represents a range of periods: from early-twentieth-century armchairs to eighteenth-century tables to 1950s bookshelves, made-to-measure by a Trieste carpenter according to a design by the architect, Gustavo Pulitzer, who renovated the house in the early post-war period. As we hinted earlier, the atmosphere is characterized by an endless number of collections: on the sitting-room coffee table we find a collection of silver boxes, nearby we find porcelain elephants, all with trunks pointing skywards, a good luck symbol; on an Empire table, on the other hand, a collection of snuffboxes, one lovelier than the next; near the fireplace, not only prestigious eighteenth-century works, but also a collection of rare antique fans. And then there are the books, that are found everywhere. On this same floor there is a dining room with a collection of Chinese works and a guest cloakroom, since the marquise loves to organize dinners and receptions.

On the first floor there is an ochre-colored antechamber with four doors that lead to the more private quarters of the house. There is the azure drawing room with such a Venetian air to it: pale blue *boiserie*, a sofa upholstered in striped jacquard, a cupboard decorated with a trompe l'oeil Arcadian scene, a console table, and small writing desks. And above all "hands": drawings, prints, watercolors, ornaments, and tiny sculptures. The bedroom is also eclectic: the bed is simple, with floral satin headboard upholstery and bedspread, with braided trimming. An eighteenth-century Neapolitan work hangs above the bed and the room is full of books, prints, ornaments, drawings, and newspapers that create a decidedly lived-in feel. But Carignani's favorite room is the bathroom. The floor and walls are in aqua green mosaic, and the same informal and comfortable atmosphere of the rest of the house can be felt here too: porcelain plates on the walls, floral fabrics, armchairs, and small consoles.

In the photo above, a corner of the garden with 1950s wrought iron planters. Facing page: the library area of the lounge. Through the door, the entrance to the villa and the stair.

The dining room is amplified by the far wall, covered in eighteenth-century mirror squares. The decor is completed by two wrought iron appliqués.

A corner of the lounge. The table holds a collection of eighteenth-century snuffboxes, one of the many collections of small objects found in this house.

Below: the guest bedroom on the upper floor with
an oak wood floor and pale blue doors and walls.
Facing page: the bedroom of the owner of the house,
with family portraits, prints, drawings, and books.

The upstairs bathroom is in shades
of dark blue and pale green. The
walls are finished in a ceramic
mosaic and are decorated with plates
and prints. Also featured are an art
deco table and a 1940s armchair.

Above: the guest bedroom in Romantic style. Below: the swimming-pool.

Design References

Paola Coin's Apartment, Milan

The owner of this Milanese house has an innate talent for furnishing interiors. She is lucky enough to own more than one in enchanting locations: Venice, Pantelleria, and Milan, in the Brera quarter. She maintains that each house communicates with the place where it is.

Here in Milan, a stone's throw from Via Solferino, one finds one of the city's liveliest quarters. The apartment is on the top floor of an early-twentieth-century building and has two views. On one side the windows look down onto the courtyard, characterized by typical old Milan *ballatoi* or landings, on the other there is the square with its handsome Romanesque church in exposed brickwork, and three chestnut trees that explode with lovely color in spring.

The house is entirely white. In contrast with the Milanese tradition that prefers wood in natural tones, the owner of the house has opted for white paint even for the floor. As a result the rooms seem much larger, a snowy container in which the items of furniture stand out. The living room includes a relaxation area, a dining area, and a library, which are carefully balanced with classical and contemporary items. The sofas are all different, including a comfortable settee of generous forms which sits next to a 1930s easy chair. The owner has asked her friend, the architect Aldo Cibic, to design several pieces.

The dining table is a modern antique; the folding metal outdoor chairs are covered in pretentious and extremely light-hearted cardinal red velvet. To play down the choice of art deco desks and consoles, there are industrial bookcases in galvanized metal loaded with art books. The kitchen, with its two french windows, is visible from this corridor. One french window leads out onto the landing and the other onto a small terrace overflowing with lavender and jasmine. The kitchen is very simple. It has no designer furniture, just a marble surface that houses the sink, a square table, and a gas stove, the famous cooker that was so fashionable in the 1950s and which, for Milan's design fanatics, is a true cult object. Opposite the kitchen we find the guest room, with a sofa bed, an elegant table, and white wood *boiserie*, which holds photographs.

The master bedroom is very large. The bed is characterized by a gigantic textile head, facing a system of curtains and mirrored walls that create an original wardrobe, while a side table and two 1950s armchairs create an informal reading corner. A door leads into the master bathroom, which looks out onto a small terrace, which is the true delight of this Milanese house.

In the photo above, a closing leaf art deco piece and in the foreground a sofa upholstered in lozenge-patterned fabric. Facing page: the dining area with an early twentieth-century table, garden chairs reinterpreted in gold and cardinal red velvet, and a Marlene Dumas triptych.

The living room is a white container. Important pieces like the Japanese panel, a lamp by the artist Andreas Schultze, 1930s-style sofas, are flanked by the informality of an industrial aluminum bookshelf. Facing page: details of the living room and the entrance.

Top: the living room. In reflecting steel, Ron Arad's armchair-sculpture.
Bottom: a 1940s armchair.
Facing page: in the bedroom an original solution is offered by a closet built into a niche and closed by a series of curtains and mirrored surfaces.

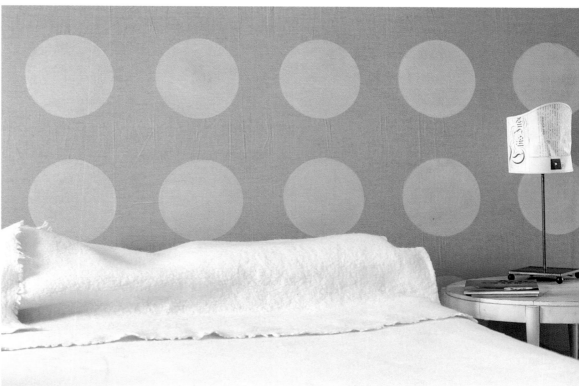

Top: the guest room. A studio couch by the architect Aldo Cibic in shades of yellow and orange. Bottom: the bedroom used by the owner of the house has a textile headboard, also by the architect Cibic. Facing page: the bathroom, with cement boiserie and 1920s taps.

Sophisticated Design

Rodolfo Dordoni's Loft, Milan

Milan is certainly the Italian city that boasts the strongest interest for modernity and for architecture by great architects. Some difficulty in the creation of contemporary architecture suited to international taste in recent years has led many of the city's inhabitants, especially the more creative, to identify unusual solutions. Former machine shops and laboratories that were present in the city from the immediate post-war period, fell into disuse and were transformed into large-scale residences. One such is that of Rodolfo Dordoni, in the Porta Genova area, located inside an old textile industrial plant. "It was the factory canteen," comments Dordoni, one of the city's top architects. "For years I had been looking for a house out in the country right outside Milan. When I saw this factory, with its huge tree-lined garden, I didn't think twice: I left the house I had in the center and abandoned the idea of a house in the country. This one was enough for me."

The restructuring took a couple of years but the result was well worth it. The space is split into two levels. On the ground floor there is a large living room, that looks out onto the garden, with sliding doors that during good weather allow continuity between the interior and the exterior. Then the kitchen, which is the continuati on of the living room, looks out onto a kitchen garden closed by jasmine and aromatic plants, as well as a mosaic tank.

A first staircase leads to the upper level of the house. This covers the kitchen and the downstairs facilities, and looks down into the living area. Here there is a library area, protected by an iron baluster, and symmetrical to the library there are two bedrooms, with a bathroom and dressing room. The house was deliberately finished with poor materials, which is required by modern architectural practice. The floor is finished with a cast of gray

cement, the walls have white plastering, and the fixtures aluminum and iron. The doors are made of wood, and the baluster is in square section iron, while the bookcases in the library and the stairs leading to it are of fir.

Dordoni has furnished the house with a series of prototype pieces that he created for the design companies with whom he works, mixing them with pieces of historic design and contemporary works of art. Thus, the general atmosphere is one of rarefied luxury thanks to the large open spaces and oversized furniture. A general sense of eclectism is evident in the choice of materials, which go from the extremely poor, like iron and raw wood, to the ultra luxurious, like leather, suede, and fur. The atmosphere is created by a play of full-length curtains in different shades that close the house and shade it from strong light on sunny days.

Above: detail of a rice paper lampshade, vases, and lamps designed by Rodolfo Dordoni. Facing page: the living room looks onto a park. In good weather the ribbon windows reduce the separation between the interior and exterior.

*The kitchen uses prototypes and industrial pieces made
by the architect. It looks out onto a closed garden whose
walls are hidden by aromatic plants and jasmine.
In the foreground several seventeeth-century Lombard
works of art resting on the floor.*

The living area is subdivided into zones. In this photo,
a table designed by Eero Saarinen in 1956 holds a series
of steel objects. On the wall, a sketch by Sol Lewit and,
beyond the column, a triptych by Gabriella Casiraghi.

The room has white walls and a cement floor.
Poufs, couches, and tables are prototypes designed
by Rodolfo Dordoni for Minotti, where he is the
art director. They alternate with older pieces.
Facing page: colored glass design by Dordoni and Sottsass.

A fir staircase leads to the upper
floor. A square section iron baluster
looks down from the library into
the large living room.

In the study area a large canvas by the young designer Gordon Guillaurmiere. Facing page: an old baroque armchair and an oil by Angelo Micheli.

The house has a number of passages
without doors. In this photo, a view
of the library seen from the bedroom.

The minimalist bathroom is a large space. Dordoni even collects works of contemporary art for his bathroom.

The Italian House: Cosmopolitanism and Tradition Converge

Palazzo Interiors

A Noblewoman's House, Venice

Legend has it that Giacomo Casanova was a visitor to the building where this Venetian apartment is located. The owner is an elegant and extremely Venetian lady, who reveals that until a few decades ago one of the balcony columns bore the signature of Giacomo, but it has sadly vanished over the years. Historically speaking, this palazzo, not far from Rialto, was built in the fifteenth century, for the marriage between a Foscari and a Mocenigo, two families strongly connected with the city's history, but now has an eighteenth-century plan following renovation.

The apartment is on the main floor of the building. It is reached via a portico with stone columns supported by small lions that are the city's symbol. The interior, covering about one thousand square feet, has a classical structure: a large *portego* used as a living room, onto which the rest of the rooms in the house open. We may start with the structure. The floor, with the exception of the *portego*, is of *terrazzo*-type tiles, in natural nuances of earth and brown. The ceiling is high, over sixteen feet, with a variety of finishes. Lacunar in natural wood in the main living room; with a gilt eighteenth-century molding in the bedrooms and in the dining room; with an eighteenth-century stucco decoration of small flowers in the drawing room.

The doors and the window frames have not been touched in any way: they all date from the 1700s, and the only poetic license conceded by the owner of the house is in the color, a powder blue used even on the radiator covers, which were made in the 1950s by a Venetian craftsman using historic drawings. The main rooms have leaded windowpanes made with small glass tondoes in colors such as aubergine, pale yellow, muted green, and antique pink. The effect of the light filtered by these windows is beautiful. The walls in the main rooms are in Venetian stucco, the colors vary from off-white to sage green and pale yellow. The technique of finishing walls in stucco actually

Above, a detail of the lounge window with its colored panes. On the facing page: the apartment's portego has been dedicated to leisure time, with a 1930s settee and numerous plants.

originated in Venice to decorate patrician mansions while defending them from the terrible dampness. Over the centuries the technique was a well-kept secret that the craftsmen handed down from father to son. It is still popular because of interest in the craft traditions. A professional application may last in excess of fifty years, as is the case in this house.

The furnishings include original antique items mixed with oriental furniture and carpets. The more valuable items include two original eighteenth-century Venetian bureaus, seventeenth-century pier-glasses in the *portego*, lacquered in blue and gold, as well as two late-eighteenth-century dressers in the dining room. The dining table is nineteenth-century Sicilian, while the chairs here are large seventeeth-century items covered in leather with dust covers. The classic style is broken by four Chinese rugs in the *portego*, a red Chinese console, and a collection of paintings by early-twentieth-century artists, including Virgilio Guidi, Felice Carena, and Bruno Saetti. There are a few knick-knacks, mainly Murano vases, including several signed by Fulvio Bianconi. Finally, in the bedroom, the headboard is made from an eighteenth-century French frieze, illuminated by an Indian silk bedspread.

Above, the walls of the main rooms are in pastel shades of Venetian stucco. On the right, the lounge window with its lead welded round colored panes. Facing page: another image of the portego, *with the terrace overlooking the canal.*

The lounge is a cleverly decorated with a mix of objects and styles. Facing page: the detail is of a red Chinese console, with an alarm clock and period vases. In the background, an early-nineteenth-century canvas.

All the rooms in the house open onto the portego. In the background the breakfast room and the barrel vault that characterizes the entrance to the house. Facing page: the headboard is made from an eighteenth-century French frieze and the walls are finished in antique pink.

Baroque *Capriccio*

Bruno Caruso's Studio in Rome

Bruno Caruso's atelier is on the top floor of a late-nineteenth-century building directly facing the Colosseum. Once inside, however, contemporaneity is left behind, since the interior is of an antique flavor and not only because of the seventeenth-century works that cover many of the walls. The study of this refined Sicilian artist, who moved to Rome many years ago, is a testament to the life of a man of art and letters, a curious intellectual who is always seeking new inspiration for his work, which is exhibited all over the world. The apartment has white walls and the turquoise floor tiles were hand-painted by the artist himself, in Moorish style. The first room is the largest in the house: a living room with comfortable sofas and many portfolios that contain not only his sketches, framed and unframed works, but also marble busts and columns used in the neoclassical manner. "Marble is a material that I truly love," comments Caruso. "I know every type and its origin."

Proof lies in the series of obelisks grouped together like a collection, and the tables made with polychromatic marble tops, designed by the artist himself.

The studio where Caruso paints is decorated with seventeenth-century art: "They are minor artists, but of excellent pictorial standard, I know how and why each one painted each work. That way I feel closer to them." A small bookcase holds art books, the artist's monographs, volumes of history and archaeology with several particularly important works purchased from Roman antique dealers, including the first edition of Alessandro Manzoni's *Storia della colonna infame*, a first edition of Cesare Beccaria's *Dei delitti e delle pene*, as well as a precious volume created by the Japanese painter Hokusai.

In the bedroom, there are more paintings, including a collection of portraits of friends: Detlef Heikamp, Mario Praz, Federico Zeri, Fabrizio Clerici, and a signed photograph of Picasso. The items of furniture are chosen to reflect the atmosphere that the artist wished to create: vintage pieces alongside contemporary furniture; all sorts and sizes of chests of drawers holding the artist's drawings, chairs that range from seventeenth-century leather and wood to the neoclassical.

But the biggest surprise is in the loft. Especially what Caruso himself actually calls "the meditation room," which houses a large number of reproductions of skulls and works dedicated to the theme of death. "I began almost by chance: I was given two skulls as a gift about forty years ago. Then from Central America I received a collection of thirty-five terra-cotta skulls. Since then my friends have always given me things on this same theme: they would get rid of it and I would take it on board."

*Another view of the studio. Here the artist uses a table
with a marble base for his drawing. As well as the
seventeenth-century oils, the room is furnished with
obelisks, columns, and a comfortable leather Chesterfield.*

*As well as his canvases, scattered throughout the studio,
there are also collections of antique books, tiles, and majolicas,
polychromatic marble, elegantly arranged by subject.*

In the studio where Caruso keeps his easels, there
are neoclassical busts, marble cups, and frames of different
shapes and sizes. Caruso loves to be surrounded by objects
that immerse him in the history of Rome.

The artist has opted to relax on a Turkish style bed,
embellished by a fur bedspread. The floor is finished
in tiles, which Caruso hand painted himself in turquoise,
and is covered by an oriental rug.

A *Dammuso* with Color

A Cosmopolitan Couple in Pantelleria, Sicily

In the photo above, the exterior of the dammuso. Unlike the others found on the island that have been extensively restructured, Gail Blacker prefers to leave the house just as she found it and has only restyled the interior of the building. Facing page: the portico with its view of the sea.

There is a house here that until thirty years ago was the home of a farming family, whose heirs had emigrated to every corner of the globe and had long since lost interest in the property. The house was spotted by a young couple: she is the American Gail Blacker, from New York, he is Sicilian, Egidio Falco, from Palermo. They decided to take the house and renovate it one step at a time. Blacker, the lady of the house, was tired of living in the fast pace of New York and could not wait to get her hands on an authentic Mediterranean ruin. Without sacrificing any of her decorating talent, she opted for minimum interventions and restored the house to its ancient aura. Part of the house's strength of character is the flooring—majolica tiles are present in different patterns and colors throughout the house. She overturned the ancient Sicilian tradition of white walls by trying out different colors to match each room. The hall is in a saffron yellow color. The room has few elements, including

a bench padded with cushions and transformed into a settee with fabric bought in the market. The same can be said for the table and a series of cushions covered in straw. The dining room is next door. Here, too, there are few furnishings, but pride of place is given to an art nouveau table bought in a Palermo antique shop, a cleaned, restored dresser credenza, and small wooden armchairs of the early twentieth century.

"With these high, star-vaulted ceilings the color creates a protective and reassuring effect. That is why, especially on the ground floor, I used the sponged color that is more usual in Arab culture, in particular in Morocco: that is another place where there is a great use of majolica and I noticed how color strengthens their impact."

Since the house had no running water inside, the kitchen and bathroom were built from scratch. In the kitchen Blacker has opted for a lead gray color that she has applied with stucco effect on the sink unit, the partition wall, and the *boiserie*. The same treatment was applied in the bathroom: the flush mounted basin unit, the wooden paneling, and the walls that close the shower are cement, colored in cardinal red. The study and the bedroom are both upstairs. Here the ceiling is lower and color alternates with white. In the study the textile panels stand out for the patchwork technique used on curtains and screens, made with antique cloth found in Sicily. In the bedroom the blue in the majolica is repeated only in the alcove that houses the bed. The furnishings are completed by a sofa covered in white gauze with a collection of cushions in velvet, and a series of recycled chairs and tables decorated with glass tessellas. No alterations were made outside except for the creation of a wood and straw portico.

The two-story house has the living
area on the first level: four rooms
with a star-vault and majolica tiles.
The owner of the house has made only
one creative intervention by coloring
the walls in Pompeii red, saffron
yellow, bright green, and ochre.

*The house has no precious furniture, only late-nineteenth-
and early-twentieth-century pieces of Sicilian craft, with
a stylish use of color and fabrics. Gail enjoys seeking out old
cloth in Sicilian markets, which she then uses to upholster
furniture and make bedspreads.*

*The study is very sparsely furnished. The floor is of raw cement
and has only one or two items of furniture, including the chest
of drawers recuperated in an old Sicilian haberdashery.
In the foreground, a child's straw chair decorated by Gail Blacker.*

The bathroom is the only place in
the house that has been newly built.
The owner has had a cement structure
built, including a shower and the base
for basin, and the boiserie. *The entire
room is painted in Pompeii red.*

The sleeping area preserves the house's historic structures with a star vault and a beautiful niche. Here the owner has opted for traditional white walls. The floor tiles in shades of sky blue, ecru, and blue stand out. Near the bed there is a decorated chair.

Top: the bed is a traditional studio couch with cloth upholstery, set in a blue-tinted niche that reflects the color of the floor. On the right, a sofa covered in fabrics decorated by the American stylist.

Time Rediscovered

An Architect's House and a Sculptor's Studio near Cremona

The house is an eighteenth-century stamp courtyard building. In the photo above, the entrance with a work by the sculptor Leone Lodi and terra-cotta planters. Facing page: Lodi's studio, which has remained intact since his death.

This is Lombardy, just an hour from Milan, in the heart of the countryside around Cremona, a territory that has always been one of agriculture and characterized by its deep sense of religion.

This is the background for this lovely house, whose roots lie deep in the seventeenth century: to be precise 1688 was the year the building was constructed. A rectangular structure, the house has a main floor, an annex, a cloister, and a lovely garden. It was originally built to house a convent for the order of Poor Claires, who stayed there until 1811, the year in which the emperor ordered all convents in the Napoleonic kingdom of Italy to be suppressed. Later the property was split up, bought and sold over the space of 100 years until the early twentieth century, when a family of local merchants arrived on the scene. Since then the house has been handed down from one generation to the next and left nearly intact.

The ground floor is made up of a sequence of rooms, one within another. Apart from the kitchen, with its *terrazzo*-type tiles, all the flooring is in early-twentieth-century hexagonal cement tiles, while the ceilings, which are over thirteen feet high, have art nouveau floral decorations by the Lombard painter Angelo Brena. Each room still has the original eighteenth-century fittings in chestnut. The severe, deep-dyed oak furniture is nineteenth-century Lombard, as are the tapestries and hangings, with accessories in wrought iron and pewter; they speak of a stern and somewhat dour Lombard taste, but are nonetheless extremely charming. Upstairs there are four, square-plan bedrooms, with frescoed ceilings and walls and Cremonese speckled terra-cotta floor. The furniture is all mid-nineteenth-century Lombard craft production.

The only intervention made by the architect and owner of the house is to the section facing the main floor. The portico, with its stone columns, has been closed, and a comfortable, glassed-in living area created, while upstairs is occupied mainly by the atelier of Leone Lodoli. In the 1960s this part of the house, which formerly housed the dormitories of convent pupils, was actually rented out to this sculptor whose plaster works have been used to embellish many of Milan's public buildings, including the Palace of Justice, the Palace of Art, and the Arlecchino cinema.

The second floor of the house was his last studio, and so far has been left untouched: even now the old master's casts are still there to prove the value and beauty of his art.

In these images the corridor of the building's piano nobile *and the stairs that lead to the rooms on the upper floor. Facing page: Lodi's studio, which has not been touched, with the plaster moulds, his works, and his extensive books collection.*

In the art nouveau dining room, floral-motif wall paper, velvet drapes, and damasks. The floor is of cement-chip floor tiles decorated with ornamental motifs.
Facing page: the architect's study area is set in an old loggia with art nouveau furniture and wicker armchairs.

The bedrooms all have pale blue walls, frescoed ceilings,
and floors in Cremonese terra-cotta, in mottled red.
The two images show a walnut bed and a detail of the room.

Classic Mélange
A House in the Old Center of Naples

In the photo above, a detail of an easy chair upholstered in floral cotton and a Beidermeyer wardrobe. Facing page: one of the art deco mirrors reflects the great drawing room. Worthy of note are the Neapolitan shutters and the sumptuous cotton drapes.

Parco Margherita, Naples's art nouveau quarter, is one of the loveliest and most popular in the city. The house, designed by the architect Patrizia Marone, is in a turn-of-the-century building. For the owner of the house, an art historian who lives there with her husband, two children, and four Burmese cats, her home is very important as she spends many hours of her day here working. The renovation was "sensitive" to the original structure. With the exception of the kitchen, which was achieved by demolishing the walls of a series of small rooms and corridors to create a larger space, the layout of the house remains unaltered. Tuning into the wavelength of her client and friend, Patrizia sought to highlight what already existed, recovering architectural elements and original materials. The oak parquet has been replaned, the brasses and burnished metal on the shutters have been polished, and the casements restored and repaired, as have the doors and handles, the cast iron radiators, and the marble fireplaces.

A daring design was made on thie walls, with the addition of French-style color, trompe-l'oeil, and stenciled decorations. The large living room is green with stencil squares that frame Piranesi prints and early-nineteenth-century academy drawings in red ochre. In the dining room a two-tone marbled décor in crimson and hazelnut creates imitation *boiserie* combined with stuccoes bought in Denmark; the study where the owner of the house spends many working hours houses not only a desk, but also a series of settees and armchairs. The walls are Pompeii red reinforced with Greek fretted stencil squares. The bedrooms have wood paneling that is painted white, while the walls are hung with French cotton. As the house is very luminous, with large windows, it needed simple draperies in bright colors. Other color schemes are: cardinal red in the living room, golden yellow in the dining room, and floral print in French cotton in the study and in the bedroom, where they match the bed. This *toile de Jouy* has also been used to upholster the armchairs throughout the house, as well as fabrics with floral motifs of oriental inspiration. Scattered on the floor, there are early-nineteenth-century kilims.

The furniture is of varying styles: an original leather Chesterfield is paired with armchairs and sofas commissioned from an upholsterer, two Louis XVI armchairs, small Biedermeier armchairs and, in a bedroom, two small armchairs. The furniture is generally antique, but chosen with eclectic taste. A bookcase with Biedermeier mirrors and a Wilhelm-period writing desk enhances the sitting room, an early 1800s English table decorates the dining room, a Biedermeier cabinet sits in the study, and a Sonnier commode completes the bedroom. By contrast the kitchen furniture is in cream enameled wood of 1940s inspiration, and the bookcase in the study area were specially designed by an architect who is a friend of the owner.

The large green living room has stencil squares and period prints pasted to the wall, which was a popular trick with nineteenth- and twentieth-century decorators. A bookcase with Beidermeier mirrors is set against the wall.

A view of the living area. A color contrast plays the green of the walls against the cardinal red used for the curtains and accessories. The floor is original oak parquet with staves laid out in herringbone pattern. In the foreground, a Louis XVI armchair.

The study walls are in Pompeii red decorated with
black Greek stencil squares. The room includes Beidermeier
and neoclassical furniture, and easy chairs with dust covers
which are changed to suit the season.

The house enjoys large windows on all four sides. A view of the study, framed by french windows with adjustable shutters.

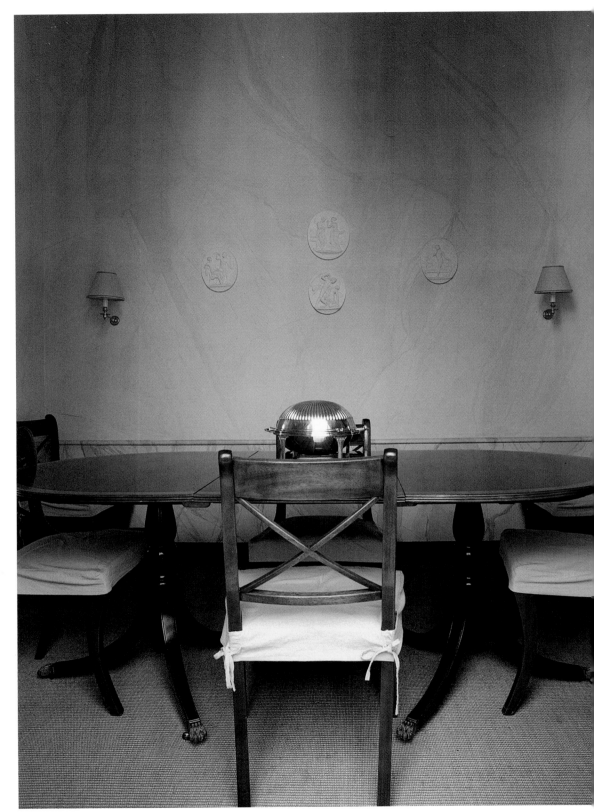

In the dining room the owners have opted for neutral shades: hazelnut for the Venetian plaster-style boiserie *and cream for the walls. Plaster medallions bought in Denmark are featured on the walls.*

The kitchen is the only renovated room in the house.
To create a single, handy space, a number of walls
were demolished. The furniture imitates kitchens from
the 1930s, in cream lacquered wood.

Seen from the Outside

A House-Garden in Pantelleria, Sicily

Pantelleria is a peasant land floating in the Mediterranean sea with tufa houses, olive groves, and vineyards. It was abandoned for centuries until it was "discovered" forty years ago by a group of friends from Milan who then proceeded to make it famous the world over. Legend has it that in the summer of 1963, when there was not yet a landing strip, just bare earth, they landed in a tiny plane. Just like in many stories where unsullied places are marked out, these friends fell in love with the island to the point that they bought several of its traditional dwellings, the *dammuso*.

Giannino Tenconi, an orthopedic surgeon and an enthusiast of opera and president of the historic foundation "Amici del Loggione" at La Scala in Milan, was one of these "discoverers." His *dammuso* faces the sea, not far from Cala dell'Elefante, one of the loveliest spots on the island. Tenconi made this his sanctuary, his *buen retiro*

where he spends many months of the year.

Over the years, what had been a simple peasant house was transformed into a wonderful home, full of comforts. All the alterations respected the principles of local architecture: the house was made of dry stone and with tufa roofs in the Arab tradition. The main *dammuso* is used as a living area: the sitting room is comprised of two sections with star vaults joined by a full arch. The ground has been laid with cement mixed as Venetian *terrazzo*, in pearl gray, with stylized floral motifs in slightly darker shades of gray. The walls are plaster-finished and some of the fixtures are metal. The furnishings are few and spartan, including a series of Central America fabrics, African statuettes, local baskets, and tables, consoles, and side tables ordered from the island's carpenter. The smaller units are used as bedrooms, each with its own small bathroom.

But the true charm of the house is outside, with its patios that connect the buildings with one another and where much of the day is spent. The garden is also beautiful and is laid out on several levels thanks to a system of stairs and dry stone walls, which also host a refined collection of tropical plants and cacti. There is a swimming pool, of course, created from natural troughs in the land, and surrounded by teak flooring. The beauty of this pool, which looks out across the sea, is the color that changes in intensity depending on the time of day, thanks to the special lining.

The house has a series of rooms that hinge around a garden arranged on a series of levels. In the photo above, the stairs that lead to the living area from the swimming pool. Facing page: the cactus garden.

The wooden porticoes are roofed with straw as is traditional on the island's houses. A lot of time is spent outdoors and these structures make it possible to create comfortable environments that offer shade from the summer heat.

The main dammuso *of the house seen from the exterior. It is set amidst rambling jasmine, palms, and dry stone walls, and is one of the oldest examples of vernacular architecture. The barrel vault keeps the inside of the house at a cool, constant temperature.*

For the interior the owner has opted for a simple, minimalist look. The floor is pigmented cement and is reminiscent of the texture of typical Venetian terrazzo flooring. The handsome vaulted walls are white plaster. Inside the house the french windows with iron fixtures are shaded by gauze curtains.

Top: the sitting room with its armchairs and sofa with white cotton dust covers, brightened by Central American textiles. Bottom: the natural cement fireplace, tinted brick red, and terra-cotta vases.

The fugue of windows shows
a part of the garden usually set for
meals. The owner of the house and
his guests enjoy dinners by lantern
light around huge teak table, serving
Sicilian fruit and delicacies.

Simple furnishings, all items
produced by Sicilian craftsmen
from whom Tenconi commissions
tables, chairs, and dressers every year.
Only one exception, early-twentieth-
century dresser in inlaid wood,
an example of turn-of-the-century
Sicilian cabinetmaking.

The swimming pool with teak staves used for the border
and with a splendid view of the sea. This dammuso is one
of the few on the island that is actually close to the coast.
Facing page: another view of the gardens with agaves and palms.

Fin de Siècle Spirit

Villa Feltrinelli on Lake Garda

In the photo above, the villa's view over the lake. The garden boasts centuries-old magnolias and lemon groves, typical of Lake Garda, known as "limonaie." Facing page: the great ramp of marble stairs that leads to the upper floors.

If houses have a soul, then this villa has a happy one. And why should it not be? It is located in one of Italy's loveliest places, at Gargnano on Lake Garda, and it has all the charm of the *fin de siècle* villas that were so fashionable in the nineteenth century. It was in fact built in 1892, a magnificent art nouveau building commissioned by the brothers Angelo and Giacomo Feltrinelli as their summer house.

The layout of the house is typical of patrician houses of that period: a central plan, with a hint of the gothic identified in the octagonal tower and the crenellations. The interior, with the lacunar ceilings and the finely made window frames, are proof of the family's original trade. In the late nineteenth century the Feltrinelli family was one of the foremost importers of wood in the kingdom of Italy. Later, Carlo Feltrinelli increased the prestige of the dynasty when he became founder and president of Edison and the Credito Italiano bank. Thanks to Giangiacomo Feltrinelli, the founder of the publishing house of the same name, the house was honored by the presence of guests such as Henry Miller and Tomasi di Lampedusa.

Today, splendor is restored to the house: after twenty-five years of abandonment, it was purchased four years ago by Bob Burns, the well-known creator of the Four Seasons Hotel in Milan. Burns turned to Pamela Babey, an American interior decorator, to transform it into a prestigious hotel with a limited number of rooms. Babey was enthusiastic when she saw the villa. The intention was to respect the strong character of the architecture and to integrate the old with the new, but in harmony.

And Villa Feltrinelli has retained its magical atmosphere. Babey and Burns wanted to restore the atmosphere of the old aristocratic house, with its library, the dining room with antique pink silk and bone china, and veranda for reading the morning's papers. The bedrooms are on the main floor and upstairs, and all have enchanting views of the lake. One fascinating room is that of the poet, which had belonged to Giangiacomo Feltrinelli, with a hexagonal layout, small porthole windows, and a centrally set bed. Another is the magnolia room on the *piano nobile*, with art nouveau frescoes and a balcony that looks out onto a centuries-old magnolia from which it takes its name. In the bathroom all technology has been abolished in favor of more traditional furnishings: old-fashioned bathtubs, retro showers with giant showerheads, and 1920s taps in nickel-plated brass, which create a much warmer and more elegant effect than steel.

The villa was built in 1892, commissioned by the brothers Angelo and Giacomo Feltrinelli as their summer residence. It is a refined example of turn-of-the-century eclectism where architectural motifs intermingle and styles of various eras are cleverly mixed. In this image, the prospect of the house seen from the piano nobile, *with the ceiling frescoed with mythological motifs and windows in colored glass.*

The square-plan hall leads into the
living area, the library, the dining
room, and the sitting room leads out
into the garden. The lacunar ceiling
is in white and gold stucco, the
marble-chip floor tiles have geometric
decorations and the walls, embellished
with strips of Venetian plaster
decoration, have niches with art
nouveau furniture and precious
mid-nineteenth-century pier-glasses.

*After years of neglect, the house was bought by Bob Burns
whose intention was to turn it into a hotel. He entrusted the
restoration to an American interior decorator, Pamela Babey,
and he asked her not to drastically change the interiors,
but rather to leave the structure as intact as possible.*

*In this photo and on the facing page, two details of the living area.
Pamela Babey's restyling has recuperated all the furnishings that
were present. The modern furniture and fittings were designed
by the stylist to blend well with the period pieces.*

Inlaid, carved wood is one of the materials that recurs most often in the house. Fortunately the structures in wood, which included ceiling paneling, door frames, and windows, as well as lacunar ceilings, were not irreparably damaged over the years and have now been restored to their original splendor.

The dining room is very handsome: the wallpaper is a floral motif,
the dresser is art nouveau, and the oval table and chairs with twisted
pillaret back and cardinal red velvet upholstery are neo-Gothic.
In the center, a Bohemian crystal candelabra with tiny fabric shades.

*The cocktail corner is next to the
reading area: the mirrored ceiling
extends the dimensions of the small space.*

A detail of the main room on the piano nobile. *The "magnolia" room boasts an ample terrace that looks out onto a centuries-old magnolia from which it takes its name. Each room has its own name: the tower room, located in the tower of the house, was the bedroom of Giangiacomo Feltrinelli, of the eponymous publishing house.*

Top: the Ave Maria room, which was the room used by Giangiacomo Feltrinelli's parents. Most of the rooms have frescoed ceilings, walls papered in soothing shades, and wooden or coconut floors. Bottom: a detail of a wardrobe door with twisted pillarets.

A general view of the "magnolia" room. The floor is the original herringbone wood parquet and the furniture is from the late nineteenth century. The lighting designed by Pamela Babey is based on table lamps scattered throughout the building to create soft ambience.

Culture on the Lagoon
A House-Foundation in Venice

Venice is a unique city. The layout of its houses is unmistakable and the same is to be said for the light, the muse that inspired great painters. Moreover, it is an international city and it attracts visitors from all over the world. Spain, for instance, has always watched Venice with great admiration. We may recall above all the eclectic persona of Mariano Fortuny, who left his own country and in this lagoon city founded one of the most prolific and fascinating schools of taste, creating the famous Fortuny style. His *plissé* fabrics and velvets are bound to the image of Venice.

Alejandro Suarez, another Spaniard like Fortuny before him, chose to live in Venice. His house in Campo Pisani, a stone's throw from the Accademia di Belle Arti, is a typical Venetian apartment: the central *portego* is a series of symmetrical rooms and on the far side has an enormous window that looks out onto the Accademia Bridge. The layout has not been touched, not even the original Venetian *terrazzo* floor. But the style of this house is not the traditional style of the city. Suarez has endowed his interventions with an international tinge that deviates from the local style with a decidedly refined taste. A truly special cosmopolitan air reigns, but with an eye to minimalism. In fact, the interior is quite empty but the limited amount of furniture and paintings are full of character. This means that the structure is enhanced and the original seventeenth-century slab mosaic flooring can be fully appreciated, a floor that some experts declare to be one of the loveliest in the city. The same can be said of the Venetian plastered walls and eighteenth-century fixtures that have been restored and repainted.

One enters through the hall created from a portion of the original *portego*. This leads to the living room, dominated by light and furnished

with a few items of designer furniture. The dining room leads off the living area and is also furnished with contemporary items, as do the bedrooms, which are the most interesting rooms in the house. They are large, which is a privilege in Venice, and they also have unusual details, such as the great niches that house a *sommier*, which Suarez himself commissioned after seeing the ottoman couches at Topkapi Palace in Istanbul. The palest green *boiserie* wardrobes and the marble and spatula finished plaster bathrooms repeat the colors used in the rooms: wisteria, Venetian green, ice blue, and magnolia. But the most beautiful feature is the piano that dominates the sitting room: in fact, the house is also the head office of the Casa de Uscoli Foundation, an homage Suarez makes to the King of Spain in Italy. On a regular basis the house organizes chamber and voice concerts, poetry, and prose readings, thus opening its doors to the Venetian public.

In the photo above, the portego, *which retains the classical structure of a Venetian house and which Alejandro Suarez has left to its original function of great hall onto which all the rooms in the house open. Facing page: the drawing room. The floor, in Venetian* terrazzo, *is one of the oldest and most intact of the city.*

The house is typically Venetian: fixtures and fittings such as doors and wooden paneling have been restored to their original state. Suarez, on the other hand, has given the house a cosmopolitan style by integrating the eighteenth-century layout with modern furniture, light colors, and contemporary art.

The house is also a foundation, Casa de Uscoli, which opens about ten times each year for art exhibitions, concerts, and small-scale congresses. In the photo we see the conference room. The ceiling has original late 1700s plaster applications, a stone fireplace with a baroque painting, and minimalist furniture.

One of the four bedrooms is a large niche with an inlaid
polychromatic wooden floor. The rest of the room has slab
mosaic paving. The bed was designed by the owner of the house
and like all the studio couches found in these rooms, it was inspired
by the canapés in Istanbul's Topkapi palace of the sultans.

The bathrooms are all new and next to the bedrooms. Unlike the rest of the house, which has white walls, various shades of Venetian stucco have been used: sea green, gray, blue, and violet.

Deco + Contemporary

Blending Styles with Two Roman Gallery Owners

If anyone was to think that Rome is a city that only favored an ostentatious Baroque style, they would be mistaken. The home of Bruno Puiatti and Giuliano Matricardi, enterprising gallery owners, is proof of that. The classic Roman house of the old center is a seventeenth-century building. The top floor dwelling begins with a small hall and a staircase that leads to the apartment above.

The house is not large. A corridor with hexagonal terra-cotta tiles opens into the living room. Then there is a dining room, a mini kitchen—fully equipped for the dinner parties the two hosts organize every month for more than thirty people, when they have a new show opening at their gallery—and a guest bathroom. Opposite the living area there is the sleeping area: on one side the bathroom and walk-in wardrobe, on the other a bedroom.

The apartment has two terraces. One is outside of the living area and houses a separate structure, which is about a century old, with inside a lovely *boiserie* in white wooden squares, which the two owners of the Il Ponte gallery have organized as a small studio and guestroom. The second terrace is reached by an iron staircase and covers the entire apartment.

Bruno and Giuliano have put together furnishings with numerous items from the 1920s and 1930s, purchased chiefly from antique shops in the center of Rome: a number of pieces are beautiful and precious, like the art deco dining-room table, the two 1920s Venetian crystal chandeliers, fitted in the center of the sitting room and the dining room. Other pieces are less important, but ideal for a comfortable mix, like the divans upholstered in white *housse*, scattered with tiger-striped cushions, the 1930s double

bed in the bedroom, played down by lace-trimmed sheets and pillows, and the 1950s armchairs upholstered in white-trimmed pink velvet. The table lamps, however, are designer items from the 50s and 70s and have in common the glass shade and metal structure.

The two gallery owners have adopted a rule regarding the art: the living area is for sculptures and paintings by Ford Beckman, Giorgio Lupatelli, and Erwin Olas; the dining room is for the photographs by Matthias Hermann, Dino Pedriali, Nitche, Annie Leibovitz, and Inez van Lamsweerde; the bedroom is for photographs and portraits by Dino Pedriali and Matteo Basilé; the guestroom is for drawings and watercolors by Carlo Maria Mariani, Cristiano Pintaldi, Nino Longobardi, and Franco Silvestro; and in the corridor, a new arrival, an installation by Maurizio Mochetti, *Aereo con Laser* [Airplane With Laser].

In the photo above, a 1930s alarm clock. Facing page: the bedroom. A 1930s bed, early-twentieth-century bedside cabinets, a pair of nineteenth-century Neapolitan fans, a crucifix in inlaid wood, and a Venetian mirror. Above the bed, a work by Matteo Basilé, titled 31.12.99.

In the dining room, the walls are hung with works of contemporary art including a portrait of Andy Warhol by Dino Pedriali and, by the same artist, a photograph of a male torso.

In the living room, two 1950s armchairs. On the walls,
Clown Portrait *by Ford Beckman and, between the two*
windows, Epistemologo *by Fabrice De Nola.*

In this photo, a detail of the guest bathroom door. Facing page: the corridor and a detail of the kitchen.

Nineteenth-Century Inspiration

Neoclassical Design in Milan

The nineteenth century is in the blood of the owners of this Milanese house. We are in the historic Lazzaretto quarter often mentioned by Alessandro Manzoni in *The Bethrothed*. About ten years ago Lino Raggio and Gianfranco Signori, creators and owners of the Sharra Pagano line of jewelry, spotted an early-twentieth-century house that was to become their home. On the top floor the attic was recovered to create an apartment. The criterion for renovating was based on the layout of a nineteenth-century house, with ample rooms that pass from one to the next and with a clear division of the kitchen and bathroom areas. On the main floor there is the entrance with a huge dining room dominated by an oak Regency table; a sliding door opens into the living room, while a passageway supported by plaster pilaster strips leads from the dining room to a small drawing room where there is a small but well-stocked video library. On the other side of the corridor, there is the kitchen,

the guest bathroom, and the laundry room. The entire house has dark oak flooring with cream-colored walls and plaster moulding at ceiling height, creating an elegant atmosphere; the doors and fixtures are in original white lacquered wood, from the early twentieth century. The dominant colors of the furnishings are the blue, which can be seen in the large Chinese rugs, the gold in the frames of most of the paintings in the house, the dark wood of the original nineteenth-century and early-twentieth-century furniture, purchased from Milan's antiques galleries. In the living room there is a pair of Napoleon III items in black and gold, surmounted by two still-lifes from the 1800s, a Bohemian crystal candelabra at the center of the room, and a console with sphinxes in Empire-style gilt stucco. In the main drawing room there are Regency sofas in black leather capitonné upholstery and nineteenth-century French paintings. Other elements include a series of late-nineteenth-century Emile Gallé vases and a series of niches housing a collection of neoclassical heads and busts.

A cream varnished, wrought-iron staircase, enhanced by plaster medallions and ecru tassels, leads to the upper floor. The second section of the house is more informal, especially the living area. In fact, most of the attic is occupied by a winter garden where the owners have placed settees upholstered in white cotton, combined with iron tables and chairs. The veranda looks out over an ample terrace, filled with climbing plants and jasmine, where many a party is organized during warm weather. The sleeping area returns to the severe style of the living area. Once again the flooring is in wood, with white walls and niches. A bed and pouf covered in simple white fabric offset a wood and glass art deco bookcase, with a refined series of Italian nineteenth-century portraits of women.

In the living room, a capitonné Chesterfield in black leather, hand-colored and decorated 1920s and 1930s Venetian vases in Murano glass, and a late-nineteenth-century portrait of a woman, Milanese school.

A detail of the small study in the house with Beidermeyer pieces and the drawing room-library dominated by an art nouveau fireplace, with a collection of Tiffany and Gallé vases.

The upstairs bedroom. The mirror on the Beidermeier
wardrobe reflects the nineteenth-century English wood
bookcase, purchased to store and protect the books.
On the right, an oil portrait of a lady, dated early twentieth
century, a small Chinese table, and a Chinese rug on the floor.

In the dining room more canvases of female subjects. A centrally hung chandelier lights the room, together with a pair of French crystal appliqués on the walls.

A cream varnished wrought iron staircase, enhanced by medallions and tassels, designed by the owners of the house, connects the piano nobile with the attic. Here the floor is in oak and the walls are partially decorated with Venetian plaster.

Upstairs a veranda has been turned into a winter garden with a number of sitting areas. The veranda and the master bedroom both lead out onto a terrace. In the photo, a detail of the attic living area, with leather settees, gilt mirrors, and plaster busts.

Baroque Dream

Roberto Lucifero's Eclectic House, Rome

Roberto Lucifero, one of Rome's most famous interior decorators, lives in this house, in the heart of Rome, a stone's throw from Campo de' Fiori. The apartment is on the top floor of a massive baroque building, but like all houses in the capital, it has been remodeled and added to over the centuries. And Lucifero's house is just such a patchwork. The entrance is through a small wooden door and a steep, narrow staircase in wood covered with antique carpet.

The room immediately declares that this is an eccentric world not embraced by the parameters of contemporaneity. The effect is that of a seventeenth-century theater where every detail is designed, set-up, decorated, and finished to create an overall effect of immense charm. This is not a single-floor apartment, but a jumbled world of rooms above one another and next to each other. Just as the magic of the theater creates a unique world with every scene, here every room develops an iconographic theme.

Let us return to the first room. This is an Arcadian drawing room with decoration and paintings on the theme. Of the various works, the largest is a Renaissance subject conceived as the cover of a book by the owner of the house, titled *Guida ai Giardini perduti di Roma* [A Guide to The Lost Gardens of Rome], a work dedicated to twenty or so patrician villas lost to posterity. The surroundings are parquet flooring with intarsia design, Renaissance pattern fabrics, and baroque armchairs and sofas. The adjoining room is the library, of Gothic inspiration. Here the books are laid out on shelves that repeat the decorated wood effect motif of the walls.

On the second floor is another drawing room and a bedroom, while the bathroom is half way up the ramp of stairs between the lower and upper floor. In the drawing room the dominant color is a strong sage green, emphasized not only by the walls but also by the furnishings, which include a *bergère* in shot velvet with long fringes and neoclassical armchairs upholstered in Guatemalan fabric. Lucifero is manually skilled and he defines himself a carpenter, joiner, maker of mosaics, and author of trompe-l'oeil. His artistic talent is seen in the wall that separates the green room from the bedroom: the access door is camouflaged in the wall by a trompe-l'oeil of a "Renaissance Bridge over a River." The bedroom reproduces classic ornamental motifs: the walls, in faded green, are applied with shells that also serve to create elements such as niches and shelves, creating an extremely unusual effect. Then, another staircase, and another room. The dining area is the most recently built. The room is inspired by an antique Company of the Indies dinner service, which is housed in two "Chinese" cabinets, mahogany display units created by Lucifero. Finally, on the top floor, there are terraces and in the center, like the cockpit of a boat, a structure in wood and glass that houses the kitchen.

In the photo above, a detail of the shell decoration used in the bedroom. Facing page: the small first floor drawing room. Roberto Lucifero has decorated every inch, from floor to ceiling, with motifs inspired by Renaissance Arcadian culture.

The house has a beautiful mix of simple and valuable objects, which the owner of the house, an internationally famous set designer and interior decorator, has combined using his own, very personal taste.

*The library next to the drawing room is of Gothic
inspiration. The books are arranged on shelves
that repeat the decorated wood effect of the walls.*

A detail of the dining area with a decorated screen, a neoclassical table, tureen, candelabra, and silver ewer. Facing page: the small drawing room next to the bedroom.

The green drawing room leads into
a faded green bedroom decorated with
baroque-inspired shell applications.

All the World's a Stage
Maestro Luciano Damiani's House and Theater in Rome

In the photo above, the corridor between the bedroom and a study. Facing page: the room Luciano Damiani uses as his chief study. The famous set designer and stage director had divided the rooms with textile panels and wings.

Is this a theater that resembles a house or a house that seems a theater? Luciano Damiani, one of Italy's masters of set design, does not see the dilemma. His house and his theater cohabit at Testaccio, one of Rome's liveliest and more populated quarters. About twenty years ago, Damiani, a set designer and director famous for his work with the Piccolo Theater and La Scala in Milan, discovered a series of barrel-vaulted grottoes at Monte dei Cocci. The grottoes were dug into the mount itself, which the Romans used from the 1600s as a warehouse for furniture and foodstuffs because of the cool, steady temperature. Damiani bought several of the grottoes to use as a storeroom for stage sets created for Rome's Teatro Argentina. To this master's eye these dark, stark chambers did not appear as they had for so many centuries and he perceived the possibility of transforming them into something totally different. They could become a theater or, better still, his own theater. After a complex operation of recovery and reconstruction

that took almost a decade, Damiani opened his Teatro di Documenti.

The theater itself is an intriguing, enchanted place, where the stage and the auditorium merge. Here the mirror effect created by the two superimposed and communicating auditoria with a shared stage and orchestra pit are only the start of Damiani's refined and startling project. Changing rooms, reception rooms, stairs, corridors: a labyrinth of spaces, one after the other all in the same shades, the same finishes, so that the interior and exterior are the same; all is performance, so the audience, depending on which work is being staged, may listen to music in a room adjacent to the orchestra without seeing it, but to hear it better, or follow the *corps de ballet* from one auditorium to the next, like the rats who followed the piper in Hamelin.

The same sensation of being wrong-footed emerges in the artist's house-studio, above the theater, in which half a century of Italian theatrical history is on display: drawings, sketches, and maquettes mix with books, documents, and awards such as the 1987 Theater Critics Prize and the Theater Silver Mask for 1996. White is the dominating color for the walls, floors, many of the fabrics, and much of the furniture. Lacquered wood is the chief material: for the creation of *boiserie*, wings that define the great living area, for the construction of small monks' cells behind a wardrobe, where the director-scenographer has made his private bedroom and bathroom, one over the other. Moreover, corridor-galleries house the precious collection of costumes designed by Damiani and worn by famous personalities of the world of literature and opera, while wooden boxes interrupt the space to house books and precious objects.

The appendix to the "Teatro dei Documenti" [Document Theater] is the director's house-studio. In this image a female statue found on the upper floor of the theater that Damiani defines an ex-voto to his life as an artist. On the floor, canvases, easels, and boxes of paints that Damiani used in his youth, when he studied with Giorgio Morandi.

The house is an archive of all the plays that Damiani has brought to the stage. In this photo, a detail of the studio with a panel that reproduces a drawing by Hokusai, used during a production of Madame Butterfly.

The house is built with the same irony and good taste used for a theatrical production.

The Document Theater comprises two overlapping sections that reflect one another. The actors and the audience move through a labyrinth created within Rome's Testaccio hill.

A single stage for two audiences. In his baroque-inspired theater, Damiani constantly creates tricks of illusion and mirrors to capture artists and spectators in an all-embracing spectacle.

In the foreground a poster from Rome's Argentino Politeama theater, hanging from one of the numerous shelving units found in Maestro Damiani's home.

The "Casa dei Documenti" [Document House] corresponds to the Document Theater and gathers together books and sketches, stored in open bookshelves, on work tables and in numerous chests of drawers.

Acknowledgements

Thanks to Liliana Artero, Associazione Casa Mollino,
Gianpaolo Barberis, Roberto Begnini, Maria Grazia Borriello,
Manuela Campari, Giuliana Carbi, Chiarastella Cattana,
Francesco Durante, Marco Ferrante, Flavia Fossa Margutti,
Anna Gambatesa, Fiora Gandolfi, Nathalie Grenon,
Susanna Legrenzi, Franco Jesurum, Stefania Miscetti,
Caterina Napoleone, Luisa Sacchi, Alejandro Suarez.
Special thanks to Fiorenza Vallino, who shared the topic
of the Italian house with great enthusiasm.